I DARE YOU TO GIVE

I DARE YOU TO GIVE

*Tapping Into God's Supernatural
Resource For Your Every Need*

Jewell Fairweather-Jones

Order this book online at www.trafford.com
or email orders@trafford.com

Most Trafford titles are also available at major online book retailers.

All scripture quotations are taken from the King James Version of the Bible.

Printed in the United States of America.

ISBN: 978-1-4669-0204-6 (sc)
ISBN: 978-1-4669-0205-3 (e)

Trafford rev. 11/17/2011

 www.trafford.com

North America & international
toll-free: 1 888 232 4444 (USA & Canada)
phone: 250 383 6864 ✦ fax: 812 355 4082

CONTENTS

DEDICATION

This book is dedicated to the body of Christ, to those who are standing at the door of the kingdom, who have professed Jesus as Savior and Lord, but have not submitted themselves under His headship.

I pray that as you read this book; there will be a divine impartation of God's Spirit, presence, and anointing upon your life, and that He will minister to you exactly where you are in your journey.

May the Lord give unto you the spirit of wisdom and revelation in the knowledge of Him, and may your understanding be enlightened; that you may know what is the hope of His calling.

I pray that you will be encouraged and empowered to seek first His kingdom and His righteousness, and dare to believe that as you keep your focus on Him, that He will do exceeding abundantly above all that you may ask or think.

May you experience life in His kingdom to the fullest. Let there be light in every area of your life.

In Jesus name!

ACKNOWLEDGEMENT

I would like to thank my Heavenly Father for entrusting me with an assignment such as this. I pray that His voice will be heard and that lives will be transformed for His glory.

To Bishop, Dr. Al Baxter:

I acknowledge and appreciate the hard work, commitment and dedication, that you have invested into God's kingdom over the years. No one can stay in ministry for as long as you have without the hand and anointing of God directing and sustaining them.

Thank you for your labour of love.

May the Lord bless you always.

To Pastor Mark Anthony Baxter:

This book was birthed through you. It's amazing what can be accomplished through the power of agreement.

Thank you for your prayers, words of encouragement, and, most of all, for believing in me. You are truly a vessel of honor!

May God bless you richly!

A special thank you to my husband, Ken Jones, and to my son, Tristan Sutherland, for your love and support.

May the Lord give you both the desires of your hearts.

INTRODUCTION

For unto us a child is born, unto us a Son is given: and the government shall be upon His shoulder: and His name shall be called Wonderful, Counsellor, The mighty God, The everlasting Father, The Prince of Peace.

Of the increase of His government and peace there shall be no end, upon the throne of David, and upon His kingdom, to order it, and to establish it with judgment and with justice henceforth even forever.

Isaiah 9: 6, 7

Chapter 1

THE GREATEST GIFT

In the beginning was the Word and the Word was with God and the Word was God (John 1:1). All things were made by Him, and without Him was not anything made that was made (John 1:3).

For God so loved the world, that He gave His only begotten Son, that whosoever believeth in Him should not perish, but have everlasting life (John 3:16). For God sent not His Son into the world to condemn the world, but that the world through Him might be saved (John 3:17).

But as many as received Him, to them gave He power to become the sons of God, even to them that believe on His name (John 1: 12).

The Father loves the Son, and has given all things into His hand. He that believes on the Son has everlasting life. In Him was life; and the life was the light of men (John 1:4).

The thief comes to steal, kill, and to destroy: I am come that they might have life, and that they might have it more abundantly (John 10:10).

And the Word was made flesh, and dwelt among us, full of grace and truth (John 1:14).

Jesus is the Way, the Truth, and the Life. No one can come to the Father except through Him (John 14:6). He is the Door, the Bread of life, the living Water, the great I AM!

He came to restore us back to the Father, to destroy the works of the devil (1John 3:8), and to deliver us from the kingdom of darkness into the kingdom of light (Col. 1:13). He came to empower us to take our rightful position in God's kingdom.

It is finished! He was wounded for our transgressions, bruised for our iniquities: the chastisement of our peace was upon Him; with His stripes we are healed (Isaiah 53:5). Jesus is the author and finisher of our faith (Heb. 12:2). He has come to give us an expected end (Jer 29:11).

For the wages of sin is death; but the gift of God is eternal life through Jesus Christ our Lord (Romans 6:23).

Christ brings grace and life to all who will believe and trust Him.

For if by one man's offense death reigned by one; much more they which receive abundance of grace and of the gift of righteousness shall reign in life by one, Jesus Christ (Romans 5:17).

And this is life eternal, that we might know thee, the ONLY true God and Jesus Christ, whom thou hast sent (John 17:3).

That we may know Him, and the power of His resurrection (Phillipians 3:10).

Chapter 2

THE POWER OF LOVE

LOVE IS THE MOST powerful force in the universe and the foundation of God's kingdom. It is life's energy, light and truth.

Agape, which is the highest form of love, means unselfish, unconditional love for another. It is unlimited, unmerited, and is of and from God, who's very nature is love. It is selfless, sacrificial, and undeserving: while we were yet sinners Christ died for us (Romans 5:8). The essence of agape love is self sacrifice, which Jesus demonstrated at the cross. Everything that God does flows out of this facet of love.

Love is patient and kind, does not envy or boast, and is not proud. It is not rude, self-seeking, easily angered, or keeps a record of wrongs. Love does not delight in evil but rejoices with the truth. It always protects, always hopes, and always perseveres. Love never fails (1 Corinthians 13: 4-13).

A new commandment I give unto you, that you love one another; as I have loved you, that you also love one another. By this shall all men know that you are My disciples, if you have love one to another (John 13: 34, 35).

Love is the defining characteristic of a Christian. It is what sets God's children apart from the world.

You are the light of the world. A city that is set on a hill cannot be hid. Neither do men light a candle, and put it under a bushel, but on a candlestick; and it gives light unto all that are in the house. Let your light so shine before men, that they may see your good works, and glorify your Father which is in heaven (Matthew 5: 14-16).

For you were sometimes darkness, but now are you light in the Lord: walk as children of the light. For the fruit of the Spirit is in all goodness and righteousness and truth; proving what is acceptable unto the Lord (Ephesians. 5: 8-10).

Whoever has My commands and keeps them is the one who loves Me. The one who love Me will be loved by My Father, and I too will love them and show Myself to them (John 14:21).

That Christ may dwell in your hearts by faith; that you, being rooted and grounded in love, may be able to comprehend with all saints what is the breadth, and length, and depth, and height; and to know the love of Christ, which passeth knowledge, that you might be filled with all the fullness of God (Ephesians 3: 17-19).

We are commanded to love the Lord with all our heart, soul, and mind. And to love our neighbor as ourselves.

Thou shalt love the Lord thy God with all thy heart, and with all thy soul, and with all thy mind. This is the first and great commandment. And the second is like unto it, Thou shalt love thy neighbour as thy self. On these two commandments hang all the law and the prophets (Matthew 22:37-40).

In Luke chapter 10: 25-29, Jesus is confronted by a lawyer, who asked Him what he must do to inherit eternal life. Jesus asked him what was written in the law, and he answered, love the Lord your God with all your heart, soul, mind and strength, and love your neighbor as yourself. Jesus agreed. The lawyer then proceeded to test Him by asking, who is my neighbor? Jesus gave the parable of the Good Samaritan as an example: *A certain man went down from Jerusalem to Jericho, and fell among thieves, which stripped him of his raiment, and wounded him, and departed, leaving him half dead. And by chance there came down a certain priest that way: and when he saw him, he passed by on the other side. And likewise a Levite, when he was at the place, came and looked on him, and passed by on the other side. But a certain Samaritan, as he journeyed, came where he was: and when he saw him, he had compassion on him, and went to him, and bound up his wounds, pouring in oil and wine, and set him on his own beast, and brought him to an inn, and took care of him. And on the morrow when he departed, he took out two pence, and gave them to the host, and said unto him, take care of him; and whatsoever thou spendest more, when I come again, I will repay thee (Luke 10: 30-35).*

Jesus then asked the lawyer which of the three proved to be a neighbor to the man who fell among the robbers. The lawyer responded, the one who showed mercy. And Jesus said to him, You go and do likewise.

We are all commanded to go and do likewise!

If a man say, I love God, and hateth his brother, he is a liar: for he that loveth not his brother whom he hath seen, how can he love God whom he hath not seen (1 John 4:20)?

He that loveth his brother abideth in the light, and there is none occasion of stumbling in him (1 John 2:10).

But I say unto you, love your enemies, bless them that curse you, do good to them that hate you, and pray for them which despitefully use you, and persecute you; That ye may be the children of your Father which is in heaven: for he maketh His sun to rise on the evil and on the good, and sendeth rain on the just and on the unjust. For if ye love them which love you, what reward have ye (Matthew 5: 44-45)?

Beloved, let us love one another: for love is of God; and everyone that loveth is born of God, and knoweth God (1Peter 1:22).

Greater love has no man than this, that a man lay down his life for his friends. You are My friends, if you do whatsoever I command you. No longer do I call you servants, for the servant does not know what his master is doing; but I have called you friends, for all that I have heard from My Father I have made known to you. You did not choose Me, but I chose you and appointed you that you should go and bear fruit and that your fruit should remain, so that whatever you ask the Father in My name, He may give it to you. These things I command you, so that you will love one another (John 15: 9-17).

The love of God is the most wonderful and powerful gift we are given. Once we accept and receive His unconditional love, we can begin to love Him and allow His love to be expressed in and through us, extending it towards others. The fulfillment of love must find an act of service to flow through.

My little children, let us not love in word, neither in tongue; but in deed and in truth (1John 3:18).

Hereby perceive the love of God, because He laid down His life for us: and we ought to lay down our lives for the brethren. But whoso hath this world's good, and seeth his brother have need, and shutteth up his bowels of compassion from him, how dwelleth the love of God in him.

We know that we have passed from death unto life, because we love the brethren. He that loveth not his brother abideth in death (1 John 3: 16,17,14).

By love serve one another (Galatians 5:13).

For even the Son of man came not to be ministered unto, but to minister, and to give His life a ransom for many (Mark 10:45).

If you keep My commandments, you shall abide in My love; even as I have kept My Father's commandments, and abide in His love. These things have I spoken unto you, that My joy might remain in you, and that your joy might be full. This is My commandment, that you love one another, as I have loved you (John 15: 10-12).

If you love Me, keep My commandments (John 14:15). If you love me, feed My sheep (John 21:15-17).

Our mandate and greatest commission in life as God's children is to love. Our success depends on it.

Chapter 3

IDENTITY IN CHRIST

THE MOMENT YOU INVITE Jesus into your heart and make Him your Savior and Lord of your life, you begin the process of becoming re-created in Him, and given His nature. You become His child and adopted into His family. You receive the abundance of grace and the gift of righteousness to enable and empower you to reign in life. You are transitioned from death to life.

Therefore if any man be in Christ, he is a new creature: old things are passed away; behold, all things are become new. And all things are of God, who hath reconciled us to Himself by Jesus Christ (2 Corinthians 5:17,18).

His Holy Spirit now lives in you, filling you with His power, the power to live this new life to the fullest.

He has given you an inheritance and has made provisions for every area of your life.

Your identity, security, worth and value are now in Him, not in who you know, how many titles you may have behind your name, where you live, what you wear, what you drive, what you look like, or your financial status. Our significance is found in Christ.

When you understand who you are in Him, and your position as a child of the King, it will enable and empower you to receive, experience, and walk in the fullness of the abundant life that Jesus paid the price for you to have.

YOU ARE:

Bought with a price	1 Cor 6:19,20
A member of Christ's body	1 Cor 12:27
Joint heir with Christ	Romans 8:17
A child of the promise	Romans 9:8
Blessed with every spiritual blessing	Eph. 1:3
Justified and Righteous	Romans 5:1
A new creation	2 Cor 5:17
An expression of the life of Christ	Col 3:4
Crucified with Christ	Gal. 2:20
Given the mind of Christ	1 Cor 2:16
God's workmanship	Eph. 2:10
A partaker of a heavenly calling	Heb 3:1
Hidden with Christ in God	Col 3:3

Given direct access to the throne   Heb 4: 14-16

Chosen of God, holy and beloved   Col 3:12

Fearfully and wonderfully made   Psalms 139:14

There is therefore now no condemnation to them which are in Christ Jesus, who walk not after the flesh, but after the Spirit. For the law of the Spirit of life in Christ Jesus hath made me free from the law of sin and death. For what the law could not do, in that it was weak through the flesh, God sending His own Son in the likeness of sinful flesh, and for sin, condemned sin in the flesh: That the righteousness of the law might be fulfilled in us, who walk not after the flesh, but after the Spirit (Romans 8:1-4).

And we know that all things work together for good to them that love God, to them who are the called according to His purpose. For whom He did foreknow, He also did predestinate to be conformed to the image of His Son, that he might be the firstborn among many brethren. Moreover whom He did predestinate, them He also called: and whom He called, them He also justified: and whom He justified, them He also glorified. What shall we then say to these things: If God be for us, who can be against us? He that spared not His own Son, but delivered Him up for us all, how shall He not with him also freely give us all things? Who shall separate us from the love of Christ? Shall tribulation, or distress, or persecution, or famine, or nakedness, or peril, or sword? We are more than conquerors through Him that loved us. For I am persuaded, that neither death, nor life, nor angels, nor principalities, nor powers, nor things present, nor things to come, nor height nor depth, nor any other creature, shall be able to separate us from the love of God, which is in Christ Jesus our Lord (Romans 8:28-39).

Chapter 4

INHERITANCE

JESUS CAME TO REINTRODUCE the Kingdom of God to us, which has been given to us as an inheritance since the creation of the world. He is the door and the entranceway to our prosperity.

I am the door of the sheep. All that ever came before me are thieves and robbers: but the sheep did not hear them. I am the door: by Me if any man enter in, he shall be saved, and shall go in and out, and find pasture. (John 10:7-9).

The Spirit itself beareth witness with our spirit, that we are the children of God: And if children, then heirs; heirs of God, and joint-heirs with Christ; if so be that we suffer with Him, that we may be also glorified together (Romans 8:16, 17).

In whom also we have obtained an inheritance, being predestinated according to the purpose of Him who worketh all things after the counsel of His own will: That we should be to the praise of His glory, who first trusted in Christ.

The Lord is my chosen portion and my cup; You hold my lot. The lines have fallen for me in pleasant places; indeed, I have a beautiful inheritance (Psalms 16: 5,6).

But as it is written, eye hath not seen, nor ear heard, neither have entered into the heart of man, the things which God hath prepared for them that love Him (I Corinthians 2:9).

Fear not little flock; for it is your Father's good pleasure to give you the kingdom (Luke 12:32).

Verily I say unto you, there is no man that hath left house, or parents, or brethren, or wife, or children, for the kingdom of God's sake, who shall not receive manifold more in this present time, and in the world to come life everlasting (Luke 18:29,30).

Then the King will say to those on His right, Come, you who are blessed by My Father, inherit the kingdom prepared for you from the foundation of the world. For I was hungry and you gave Me food, I was thirsty and you gave Me drink, I was a stranger and you clothed Me, I was sick and you visited Me, I was in prison and you came to Me. Then the righteous will answer Him, saying, Lord, when did we see You hungry and feed You, or thirsty and give You drink? And when did we see You a stranger and welcome You, or naked and clothe You? And when did we see You sick or in prison and visit You? And the King will answer them, Truly, I say to you, as you did it to one of the least of these My brothers, you did it to Me (Matthew 25:34-40).

For all the promises of God in Him are yea, and in Him amen, unto the glory of God by us (2 Corinthians 1:20).

God's kingdom is one of power, promise and abundant supply, we must claim it and receive it by faith.

Chapter 5

KINGDOM LIVING

LIFE IN GOD'S KINGDOM is very different from the world's system. The principles don't always make sense to the natural mind, but are essential to living a victorious life in Christ.

The Bible tells us that in order to be first, we must be last; if we want to lead, we should serve, to receive, we must first give, and to truly live, we must die.

DIE TO SELF

For whoever will save his life shall lose it; but whoever shall lose his life for My sake and the gospel's, the same shall save it (Mark 8:35).

If any man will come after Me, let him deny himself, and take up his cross daily, and follow Me (Luke 9:23).

Verily, verily, I say unto you, except a corn of wheat fall into the ground and die, it abideth alone; but if it die, it bringeth forth much fruit. He that loveth his life shall lose it; and he that hateth his life in this world shall keep it unto life eternal. If any man serve Me, let him follow Me; and where I am, there shall also my servant be: if any man serve Me, him will My Father honour (John 12: 24-26).

I am crucified with Christ: nevertheless I live; yet not I, but Christ liveth in me: and the life which I now live in the flesh I live by the faith of the Son of God, who loved me, and gave himself for me (Galatians 2:20).

Know ye not that your body is the temple of the Holy Ghost which is in you, which ye have of God, and ye are not your own? For ye are bought with a price: therefore glorify God in your body, and in your spirit, which are God's (1 Corinthians 6: 19,20).

A yielded and surrendered life to Christ is required if we are to experience the abundant life. Those who are willing to accept, trust and obey Him, are given power to become children of God (John 1:12).

Not every one that saith unto Me, Lord, Lord, shall enter into the kingdom of heaven; but he that doeth the will of My Father which is in heaven (Matthew 7:21).

And why call Me, Lord, Lord, and do not the things which I say (Luke 6:46)?

Those who refuse to live by God's standards will be refused entrance (1 Corinthians 6:9,10). (Galatians 5:19-21).

NEW BIRTH

Repent ye; for the kingdom of heaven is at hand (Matthew 3:2).

Repent means to turn around, to change direction, to reject the kingdom of darkness and make Jesus the Lord of your life.

Jesus said, I am the light of the world; he that followeth Me shall not walk in darkness, but shall have the light of life (John 8:12).

Except a man be born again, he cannot see the kingdom of God (John 3:3). Except a man be born of the water and of the Spirit, he cannot enter into the kingdom of God (John 3:5).

Baptism is symbolic of Jesus' death, burial and resurrection. It represents dying to the old life and being raised into a new life with Christ. It is an outward demonstration of a crucified life with Christ (Romans 6:4).

Through faith in Christ we gain access into the kingdom, and our obedience positions us to receive the promises within.

For the kingdom of God is not meat and drink; but righteousness, and peace, and joy in the Holy Ghost (Romans 14:17). It is not in word, but in power (1Corinthians 4:20).

The Kingdom of heaven is where God reigns. It is where His will is done. It is where we serve Him and not ourselves. It is where we submit to Him completely. The kingdom of heaven is within you. God's kingdom is established in the hearts of His people.

The kingdom of God cometh not with observation: Neither shall they say, Lo here! Or lo there! For, behold, the kingdom of God is within you (Luke 17:20-21).

In this was manifested the love of God toward us, because that God sent His only begotten Son into the world, that we might live through Him (1John 4:9).

And that He died for all, that they which live should not henceforth live unto themselves, but unto Him which died for them, and rose again. Therefore if any man be in Christ, he is a new creature: old things are passed away; behold, all things are become new. And all things are of

God, who hath reconciled us to Himself by Jesus Christ, and hath given to us the ministry of reconciliation; To wit, that God was in Christ, reconciling the world unto Himself not imputing their trespasses unto them; and hath committed unto us the word of reconciliation. Now then we are ambassadors for Christ (2 Corinthians 15, 17-20).

Seeking God's kingdom should be our highest priority.

Seek ye first the kingdom of God, and His righteousness; and all these things shall be added unto you (Matthew 6:33).

Strive to enter in at the strait gate: for many, I say unto you, will seek to enter in, and shall not be able (Luke 13:24).

Enter ye in at the strait gate: for wide is the gate, and broad is the way, that leadeth to destruction, and many there be which go in thereat: Because strait is the gate, and narrow is the way, which leadeth unto life, and few there be that find it (Matthew 7:14).

I call heaven and earth to record this day against you, that I have set before you life and death, blessing and cursing: therefore choose life, that both thou and thy seed may live: That thou mayest love the Lord thy God, and that thou mayest obey His voice, and that thou mayest cleave unto Him: for He is thy life, and the length of thy days: that thou mayest dwell in the land which the Lord sware unto thy fathers, to Abraham, to Isaac, and to Jacob, to give them (Deut 30:19).

CREATED TO DO HIS WILL

Thou art worthy, O Lord, to receive glory and honour and power: for thou hast created all things, and for thy pleasure they are and were created (Rev 4:11).

I beseech you therefore, brethren, by the mercies of God, that ye present your bodies a living sacrifice, holy, acceptable unto God, which is your reasonable service. And be not conformed to this world: but be ye transformed by the renewing of your mind, that ye may prove what is that good, and acceptable, and perfect, will of God (Romans 12:1,2).

The word which came to Jeremiah from the Lord, saying, Arise, and go down to the potter's house, and there I will cause thee to hear My words. Then I went down to the potter's house, and, behold, he wrought a work on the wheels. And the vessel that he made of clay was marred in the hand of the potter: so he made it again another vessel, as seemed good to the potter to make it. Then the word of the Lord came to me, saying, O house of Israel, cannot I do with you as this potter? Saith the Lord. Behold, as the clay is in the potter's hand, so are ye in mine hand, O house of Israel (Jeremiah 18:1-6).

He is the potter, we are the clay. We belong to Him. We were bought with a price (1Corinthians 6:20). God wants to accomplish His will in and through us. It is up to Him to mold, transform and sanctify us.

We are created by Him, and for Him. Created to do His perfect will. We will never be fulfilled until we are doing that which we were created to do. His will provides us with purpose and direction.

As we empty ourselves of "self", then we can become the authentic vessel the Lord has created us to be. He can then fill us with His power, glory, and anointing.

Many are called, but few are chosen. The chosen one's are those who choose to do the Father's will.

Jesus answered and said unto him, who is My mother? And who are My brethren? And He stretched forth His hand toward His disciples, and said, behold, My mother and brethren! For whosoever shall do the will of My Father which is in heaven, the same is My brother, and sister, and mother (Matthew 12:48-50).

My mother and My brethren are these which hear the word of God, and do it (Luke 8:21).

Jesus was always about His Father's business. He always demonstrated the will of God. He made it clear that His life was about doing what His Father wanted Him to do.

My meat is to do the will of Him that sent Me and to finish His work (John 4: 34).

Jesus did what His Father wanted Him to do, instead of His own will. His relationship with the Father was such that He only wanted the things His Father wanted.

I and My Father are One (John 10:30). Two cannot walk unless they agree (Amos 3:3).

I must be about My Father's business (Luke 2:49)!

Jesus lived to accomplish the will of God. We are also called to accomplish His will.

It pleases God when we do His will.

And lo a voice from heaven, saying, This is My beloved Son, in whom I am well pleased (Matthew 3:17).

Blessed is that servant, whom his lord when he cometh shall find so doing (Luke 12:43).

LED BY HIS SPIRIT

All who desire the Lord's best should seek to live a Spirit-led life.

For as many as are led by the Spirit of God, they are the sons of God (Romans 8:14).

But if ye be led of the Spirit, ye are not under the law (Galatians 5:18).

The Holy Spirit is our helper, comfortor, and counselor, and guides us into all truth. He will teach us all things pertaining to living the fruitful power filled life that God intended for us to walk in.

If we live in the spirit, let us also walk in the spirit (Galatians 5: 25).

And I pray the Father, and He shall give you another comfortor, that He may abide with you forever. Even the Spirit of truth; whom the world cannot receive, because it seeth Him not, neither knoweth Him: but ye know Him; for He dwelleth with you, and shall be in you. I will not leave you comfortless: I will come to you (John 14: 16-18).

We can know God and have an intimate relationship with Him through the Holy Spirit. As we spend quality time in His presence through prayer, meditation, reading and studying His word, we will become empowered, strengthened, and developed. Our faith will increase as we become more sensitive to the Holy Spirit, hearing God's voice, and being obedient to His leading.

God's children that have His Spirit also hear His voice.

My sheep hear My voice, and I know them and they follow Me (John 10:27.

Faith comes by hearing, and hearing by the word of God (Romans 10:17).

But without faith it is impossible to please Him: for he that cometh to God must believe that He is, and that He is a rewarder of them that diligently seek Him (Hebrews 11:6).

The just shall live by faith (Habakkuk 2:4).

Faith is the substance of things hoped for, and the evidence of things not seen (Heb 11:1).

Faith is simply trusting, believing and having confidence in God. It is having confidence in His word. When God speaks a word to your heart He does not want you to doubt, no matter how things may appear in the natural.

O thou of little faith, wherefore didst thou doubt (Matthew 14:31).

For we walk by faith, not by sight (2 Corinthians 5:7).

If they obey and serve Him, they shall spend their days in prosperity, and their years in pleasures (Job 36:11).

And I will put My Spirit within you, and cause you to walk in My statutes, and ye shall keep My judgments, and do them (Ezekiel 36:27).

That the blessing of Abraham might come on the Gentiles through Jesus Christ; that we might receive the promise of the Spirit through faith (Galatians 3:14).

Howbeit when He, the Spirit of truth, is come, He will guide you into all truth: for He shall not speak of Himself; but whatsoever he shall hear, that shall He speak: and He will shew you things to come.

But the anointing which ye have received of Him abideth in you, and ye need not that any man teach you: but as the same anointing teacheth you of all things, and is truth, and is no lie, and even as it hath taught you, ye shall abide in Him (1 John 2:27).

Now we have received, not the spirit of the world, but the spirit which is of God; that we might know the things that are freely given to us of God (1 Corinthians 2:12).

FOLLOW ME

Verily, Verily, I say unto thee, when thou wast young, thou girdest thyself, and walkedst whither thou wouldest: but when thou shalt be old, thou shalt stretch forth thy hands, and another shalt gird thee, and carry thee whither thou wouldest not (John 21:18).

Follow Me, and I will make you fishers of men (Matthew 4:19).

Know ye that the Lord He is God: It is He that has made us, not we ourselves; we are His people, and the sheep of His pasture (Psalms 100:3).

And they straightway left their nets, and followed Him (matthew 4:20).

The Lord will anoint and empower you to do that which He has called you to do. He will make you into what He wants you to be. He has created us all with a divine purpose. All of God's children are gifted to establish and advance His kingdom here on earth.

God is looking for willing and obedient vessels. He is not looking for ability; He is looking for availability.

He knows our strengths and weaknesses; abilities and limitations.

Before I formed thee in the belly I knew thee; and before thou camest forth out of the womb I sanctified thee (Jeremiah 1:5).

And they said, is not this Jesus, the son of Joseph, whose father and mother we know? How is it then that he saith, I came down from heaven (John 6:42)?

The people who grew up with Jesus, who knew of His past, could not accept Him as Lord and Savior. They were too familiar with Him.

God offers us a new life, future and identity in Him. We are not defined or limited by our past. He can use the least likely person who will avail themselves to do His will.

He will choose the foolish things of the world to confound the wise; and the weak things of the world to confound the things which are mighty that no flesh should glory in His presence (1 Corinthians 1:27-29).

The wisdom of this world is foolishness with God (1Corinthians3:19).

Let no man deceive himself. If any man among you seemeth to be wise in this world, let him become a fool, that he may be wise (1Corinthians 3:18).

For every one that exalteh himself shall be abased; and he that humbleth himself shall be exalted (Luke 18:14).

The race is not to the swift, nor the battle to the strong (Ecclesiastes 9:11).

What is man, that thou art mindful of him (Psalms 8:4).

Let no man glory in men (1Corinthians 3:21).

Where wast thou when I laid the foundations of the earth (Job 38:4)?

Who has put wisdom in the inward parts? Or who hath given understanding to the heart (Job 38:36)?

We are God's hands and feet, Ambassadors of His government, who are called to represent and demonstrate His rule here on earth.

Every man shall receive his own reward according to his own labour. For we are labourers together with God: Ye are God's husbandry, ye are God's building. (1Corinthians 3: 8-9).

I have this day set thee over the nations and over the kingdoms, to root out, and to pull down, and to destroy, and to throw down, to build and to plant (Jeremiah 1:10).

And thine ears shall hear a word behind thee, saying, This is the way, walk ye in it (Isaiah 30: 21).

He who has ears to hear, let him hear (Mark 4:9).

CREATED TO BE FRUITFUL

And God said, let Us make man in Our own image, after Our own likeness (Genesis 1:26).

God blessed them and said, Be fruitful and multiply, and replenish the earth, and subdue it: and have dominion over the fish of the sea, and over the fowl of the air, and over every living thing that moveth upon the earth (Genesis 1:26-28).

And God saw everything that He had made, and, behold, it was very good (Genesis 1:31).

The Lord God took the man, and put him into the garden of Eden to dress it and keep it (Genesis 2:15).

We are created to be fruitful. Created with power, authority, responsibility and purpose. Created in the very image and likeness of our creator. God is a God of progress. In Him we live, move, and have our being. In Him we only move upward and forward, moving to higher heights and deeper depths. We are programmed for increase, and anointed to prosper in every aspect of our lives.

We are commanded to bear much fruit, abiding fruit:

Every good tree bringeth forth good fruit; Every tree that bringeth not forth good fruit is hewn down, and cast into the fire (Matthew 7:17,19).

Every branch in me that beareth not fruit He taketh away: and every branch that beareth fruit, He purgeth it, that it may bring forth more fruit (John 15:2).

Fruit is the evidence of our faith and obedience. Faith works by love (Galatians 5:6). Faith without works is dead. For as the body without the spirit is dead, so faith without works is dead also (James 2:26).

Faith must be applied in order for it to be effective.

If you have faith as a grain of mustard seed, ye shall say unto this mountain, remove hence to yonder place; and it shall remove; and nothing shall be impossible unto you (Matthew 17:20).

Our obedience will always change our season.

Giving all diligence, add to your faith virtue, to virtue knowledge, to knowledge self-control, to self-control perseverance, to perseverance godliness, to godliness brotherly kindness, and to brotherly kindness love. For if these things are yours and abound, you will be neither barren nor unfruitful in the knowledge of our Lord Jesus Christ (2 Peter 1:5-8).

That Christ may dwell in your hearts by faith; that ye, being rooted and grounded in love, may be able to comprehend with all saints what is the breadth, and length, and depth, and height; and to know the love of Christ, which passeth knowledge, that ye might be filled with all the fullness of God.

When we abide in God's word and have the word abide in us, we will produce fruit.

Being fruitful is comprehensive: spiritually, mentally, emotionally, physically, materially and financially.

We cannot produce good fruit apart from the vine. We must stay connected to the Source.

I am the true Vine, and My Father is the husbandman. Every branch in Me that beareth not fruit he taketh away: and every branch that beareth fruit, he purgeth it, that it may bring forth more fruit.

Now ye are clean through the word which I have spoken unto you.

Abide in Me, and I in you, As the branch cannot bear fruit of itself, except it abide in the vine; no more can ye, except ye abide in Me.

I am the vine, ye are the branches: he that abideth in Me, and I in him, the same bringeth forth much fruit: for without Me ye can do nothing.

If ye abide in Me, and My words abide in you, ye shall ask what ye will, and it shall be done unto you. Herein is My Father glorified, that ye bear much fruit; so shall ye be My disciples (John 15:1-8).

God's word is good seed and will always produce when the soil of our hearts is fertile, and capable of receiving. The fruit of the Spirit (Galatians 5: 22-23): love, joy, peace, longsuffering, gentleness, goodness, faith, meekness and temperance, should also be evident in our growth as believers.

In Luke 8:11-15,18, Jesus explains the parable of the sower:

The seed is the word of God. Those by the way side are they that hear; then cometh the devil, and taketh away the word out of their hearts, lest they should believe and be saved. They on the rock are they which, when they hear, receive the word with joy; and these have no root, which for a while believe, and in time of temptation fall away. And that which fell among thorns are they, which, when they have heard, go forth, and are choked with cares and riches and pleasures of this life, and bring no fruit to perfection.

But that on the good ground are they, which in an honest and good heart, having heard the word, keep it, and bring forth fruit with patience.

Take heed therefore how ye hear: for whosoever hath, to him shall be given; and whosoever hath not, from him shall be taken even that which he seemeth to have.

The parable of the talents (Mathew 25:14-30), shows that everyone is called to do their best for God. We must wisely invest what the Lord has entrusted us with i.e. our giftings, ability, finances etc. When we are faithful with a little, He will give us more. God pours into us to pour out of us. We are blessed to be a blessing.

To live in abundance we must move beyond fear, and step into a place of possibility and increase, which is what the Lord expects of us. The Lord expects us to come into the fullness of who He has created us to be. He is glorified when we bear much fruit. When we glorify God He rejoices with us. We are created to show forth His glory.

And he shall be like a tree planted by the rivers of water, that bringeth forth fruit in his season; his leaf also shall not wither; and whatsoever he doeth shall prosper (Psalm 1:3).

Chapter 6

KINGDOM GIVING

THE EARTH IS THE Lord's, and the fullness thereof; the world, and they that dwell therein (Psalms 24:1).

The silver is Mine and the gold is Mine, saith the Lord of hosts (Haggai 2:8).

If I were hungry I would not tell thee: for the world is Mine and the fullness thereof (Psalms 50:12).

Who hath prevented Me that I should repay him? Whatsoever is under the whole heaven is Mine (Job 41:11)

Thine, O Lord, is the greatness, and the power, and the glory, and the victory, and the majesty: for all that is in the heaven and in the earth is thine; thine is the kingdom, O Lord, and thou art exalted as head above all.

Both riches and honour come of thee, and thou reignest over all; and in thine hand is power and might; and in thine hand it is to make great, and to give strength unto all (1 Chronicles 29:11,12).

O Lord our God, all this store that we have prepared to build thee an house for thine holy name cometh of thine hand, and is all thine own.

I know also, my God, that thou triest the heart, and hast pleasure in uprightness. As for me, in the uprightness of mine heart I have willingly offered all these things: and now have I seen with joy thy people, and prepare their heart unto thee (1Chronicles 29: 16,17).

Thus saith God the Lord, He that created the heavens, and stretched them out; He that spread forth the earth, and that which cometh out of it; He that giveth breath unto the people upon it, and spirit to them that walk therein: I the Lord have called thee in righteousness, and will hold thine hand, and will keep thee, and give thee for a covenant of the people, for a light of the Gentiles;
To open the blind eyes, to bring out the prisoners from the prison, and them that sit in darkness out of the prison house.

I am the Lord: that is My name: and My glory will I not give to another, neither my praise to graven images (Isaiah 42: 5-8).

Now therefore, if ye will obey My voice indeed, and keep my covenant, then ye shall be a peculiar treasure unto Me above all people: for all the earth is Mine (Exodus 19:5).

All that we have and all that we are belongs to God. We are stewards of what He entrusts to us. Our gifts, ability, time, resources and finances should all be used for His glory and for His purposes. Nothing should be held tightly in our hands. It should all be surrendered to Him at His leading.

For we brought nothing into this world, and it is certain we can carry nothing out (1 Timothy 6:7).

GIVE

For God so loved the world, that He gave His only begotten Son, that whosoever believeth in Him should not perish, but have everlasting life (John 3:16).

God is loving, kind, gracious and giving. He gave out of His great love for us. He commendeth His love towards us, in that, while we were yet sinners, Christ died for us (Romans 5:8).

God sowed Jesus as a seed and sent Him forth to be multiplied and increased in and through us. When you love, you give. It is an automatic and natural response.

After Zacchaeus had a personal encounter with Jesus (love), he was transformed. He felt compelled, motivated, and inspired to give and also to repay that which he had taken dishonestly. God's grace will empower you to give.

And Zacchaeus stood, and said unto the Lord; Behold, Lord, the half of my goods I give to the poor; and if I have taken any thing from any man by false accusation, I restore him fourfold (Luke 19:8).

Blessed is he that considereth the poor: the Lord will deliver him in time of trouble. The Lord will preserve him, and keep him alive, and he shall be blessed upon the earth: and thou wilt not deliver him unto the will of his enemies (Psalms 41: 1,2).

He that hath pity upon the poor lendeth unto the Lord; and that which he hath given will He pay him again (Prov 19:17).

He that giveth unto the poor shall not lack: but he that hideth his eyes shall have many a curse (Proverbs 28:27).

Give, and it shall be given unto you; good measure, pressed down, and shaken together, and running over, shall men give into your bosom. For with the same measure that ye mete withal it shall be measured to you again (Luke 6:38).

Verily I say unto you, Inasmuch as ye have done it unto one of the least of these my brethren, ye have done it unto Me (Matthew 25:40).

The word poor means to lack, to be without, to be needy, impoverished and insufficient.

God takes pleasure in the prosperity of His children. He desires to meet needs and express His love in and through us. Everyone has a need, whether it be, mental, physical, spiritual, material or financial. *Let them shout for joy, and be glad, that favour My righteous cause: yea, let them say continually, Let the Lord be magnified, which hath pleasure in the prosperity of His servant (Psalms 35:27).*

Beloved, I wish above all things that thou mayest prosper and be in health, even as thy soul prospereth (3 John 1:2).

The Spirit of the Lord God is upon me; because the Lord hath anointed me to preach good tidings unto the meek; He hath sent me to bind up the broken hearted, to proclaim liberty to the captives, and the opening of the prison to them that are bound; To proclaim the acceptable year of the Lord, and the day of vengeance of our God; to comfort all that mourn; To appoint unto them that mourn in Zion, to give unto them beauty for ashes, the oil of joy for mourning, the garment of praise for the spirit of heaviness; that they might be called trees of righteousness, the planting of the Lord, that He might be glorified (Isaiah 61:1-3).

God is looking for willing and available vessels that He can send forth to be an expression of His love, to be the answer to someone's prayer. Our hearts cry should be, here am I Lord, send me, use me!

Therefore said He unto them, the harvest truly is great, but the labourers are few: pray ye therefore the Lord of the harvest, that He would send forth labourers into His harvest (Luke 10:2).

Say not ye, There are yet four months, and then cometh harvest? Behold, I say unto you, lift up your eyes, and look on the fields; for they are white already to harvest (John 4:35).

SOWING AND REAPING

The principle of sowing and reaping is a spiritual law that governs God`s kingdom.

Be not deceived; God is not mocked: for whatsoever a man soweth, that shall he also reap. For he that soweth to his flesh shall of the flesh reap corruption; but he that soweth to the spirit shall of the spirit reap life everlasting.

But this I say, he which soweth sparingly shall reap also sparingly; and he which soweth bountifully shall reap also bountifully. Every man according as he purposeth in his heart, so let him give; not grudgingly, or of necessity: for God loveth a cheerful giver. And God is able to make all grace abound toward you; that ye, always having all sufficiency in all things, may abound to every good work (2 Corinthians 9:6-8).

And every one that hath forsaken houses, or brethren, or sisters, or father, or mother, or wife, or children, or lands, for My name's sake, shall receive an hundredfold, and shall inherit everlasting life (Mathew 19: 29).

For we are His workmanship, created in Christ Jesus unto good works, which God hath before ordained that we should walk in them (Eph. 2:10).

Let us not be weary in well doing: for in due season we shall reap, if we faint not (Galatians 6:7-9).

I have been young, and now am old; yet have I not seen the righteous forsaken, nor his seed begging bread. He is ever merciful, and lendeth; and his seed is blessed (Psalms 37:25,26).

Cast thy bread upon the waters: for thou shalt find it after many days (Ecclesiastes 11:1).

They that sow in tears shall reap in joy. He that goeth forth and weepeth, bearing precious seed, shall doubtless come again with rejoicing, bringing his sheaves with him (Psalms 126:5-6).

The eyes of all wait upon thee; and thou givest them their meat in due season (Psalms 145:15).

To everything there is a season, and a time to every purpose under the heaven (Ecclesiastes 3:1).

God operates in time and seasons. There is an appropriate, and a set determined time for everything. We cannot rush God. His timing is always the best for us. It is to our benefit to wait on His appointed time.

Rest in the Lord, and wait patiently for Him (Psalm 37:7).

I had fainted, unless I had believed to see the goodness of the Lord in the land of the living. Wait on the Lord: be of good courage, and He shall strengthen thine heart (Psalms 27: 13,14).

While the earth remaineth, seed time and harvest shall not cease (Genesis 8:22).

INVESTING IN GOD'S KINGDOM

There is great value in investing and advancing God's kingdom. God's will is to establish here on earth what is already established in heaven.

Thy kingdom come. Thy will be done in earth as it is in heaven (Matthew 6:10).

If ye then be risen with Christ, seek those things which are above, where Christ sitteth on the right hand of God.

Set your affection on things above, not on things on the earth (Colossians 3: 1-2)

Seek ye first the kingdom of God, and His righteousness; and all these things shall be added unto you (Matthew 6:33).

For your Father knoweth what things ye have need of, before ye ask Him (Mathew 6:8).

Lay not up for yourselves treasures upon earth, where moth and rust doth corrupt, and where thieves break through and steal: But lay up for yourselves treasures in heaven, where neither moth nor rust doth corrupt, and where thieves do not break through nor steal. For where your treasure is there will your heart be also (Matthew 6:19-20).

And above all these things put on charity (love), which is the bond of perfectness.

And let the peace of God rule in your hearts, to the which also ye are called in one body; and be ye thankful.

And whatsoever ye do in word or deed, do all in the name of the Lord Jesus, giving thanks to God and the Father by Him.

And whatsoever you do, do it heartily, as to the Lord, and not unto men; knowing that of the Lord ye shall receive the reward of the inheritance: for ye serve the Lord Christ (Colossians 3: 14-15, 23-24).

Peter saith unto Him, thou shalt never wash my feet. Jesus answered him, If I wash thee not, thou hast no part with me (John 13:8).

For even the Son of man came not to be ministered unto, but to minister, and to give His life a ransom for many (Mark 10: 45).

THE HOUSEHOLD OF FAITH

For with the heart man believeth unto righteousness; and with the mouth confession is made unto salvation. For the scripture saith, whosoever believeth on Him shall not be ashamed. For whosoever shall call upon the name of the Lord shall be saved (Romans 10: 10,13).

How then shall they call on Him in whom they have not believed? And how shall they believe in Him of whom they have not heard? And how shall they hear without a preacher? And how shall they preach, except they be sent? As it is written, how beautiful are the feet of them that preach the gospel of peace, and bring glad tidings of good things! (Romans 10:14,15).

Faith cometh by hearing, and hearing by the word of God (Romans 10:17).

And He gave some, apostles, and some, prophets; and some, evangelists; and some, pastors and teachers; for the perfecting of the saints, for the work of the ministry, for the edifying of the body of Christ:

Till we all come in the unity of the faith, and of the knowledge of the Son of God, unto a perfect man, unto the measure of the stature of the fullness of Christ: That we henceforth be no more children, tossed to and fro, and carried about with every wind of doctrine, by the sleight of men, and cunning craftiness, whereby they lie in wait to deceive;

But speaking the truth in love, may grow up into Him in all things, which is the head, even Christ: From whom the whole body fitly joined together and compacted by that which every joint supplieth, according to the effectual working in the measure of every part, maketh increase of the body unto the edifying of itself in love (Ephesians 4:11-16).

And we beseech you, brethren, to know them which labour among you, and are over you in the Lord, and admonish you; And to esteem them very highly in love for their work's sake. (I Thes 5: 12,13).

Let the elders that rule well be counted worthy of double honour, especially they who labour in the word and doctrine. The labourer is worthy of his reward (1 Timothy 5:17,18).

Obey them that have the rule over you, and submit yourselves: for they watch for your souls, as they that must give account, that they may do it with joy, and not with grief: for that is unprofitable for you (Hebrews 13:17).

Remember them that are in bonds, as bound with them; and them which suffer adversity, as being yourselves also in the body (Hebrews 13:3).

With all lowliness and meekness, with longsuffering, forbearing one another in love (Ephesians 4:2).

Be devoted to one another in brotherly love. Honour one another above yourselves (Romans 12:10).

Let nothing be done through strife or vainglory; but in lowliness of mind let each esteem other better than themselves (Philippians 2:3).

And as ye would that men should do to you, do ye also to them likewise (Luke 6:31).

As we have therefore opportunity, let us do good unto all men, especially unto them who are of the household of faith (Galatians 6:10).

God has called and raised up leaders, who have dedicated their lives to Him and to the work of the kingdom. He uses them as instruments to bless, edify, encourage, strengthen, and to bring deliverance and provision to the body of Christ. He changes lives through them. They are His representatives. When we honour these leaders it pleases God. As we do good unto them, we are also doing good as unto the Lord.

A good man out of the good treasure of his heart bringeth forth that which is good (Luke 7:45).

And I myself also am persuaded of you, my brethren, that ye also are full of goodness, filled with all knowledge, able also to admonish one another (Romans 15:14).

We then that are strong ought to bear the infirmities of the weak, and not to please ourselves. Let every one of us please his neighbor for his good to edification. For even Christ pleased not Himself (Romans 15:1-3).

GIVE THANKS

The Lord is good to all: and His tender mercies are over all His works (Psalms 145:9).

We have all received from the hand of the Lord. He is gracious to everyone. He is a giving God, that's His nature. He rains on the just and the unjust (Mathew 5:45). We have so much to be thankful for: Salvation, deliverance, restoration, guidance, mercy, grace, kindness . . . for all His marvelous works.

Many, O Lord my God, are thy wonderful works which thou hast done, and thy thoughts which are to us-ward: they cannot be reckoned up in order unto thee: if I would declare and speak of them, they are more than can be numbered (Psalm 40:5).

Bless the Lord, O my soul, and forget not all His benefits (Psalms 103:2).

Every good and perfect gift is from above, and cometh down from the Father of lights (James 1:17).

The blessing of the Lord, it maketh rich, and He addeth no sorrow with it (Proverb 10:22).

If ye then, being evil, know how to give good gifts unto your children, how much more shall your Father which is in heaven give good things to them that ask Him (Mathew 7:11).

O give thanks unto the Lord for He is good. His mercy endures forever (Psalms 136:1).

Enter into His gates with thanksgiving, and into His courts with praise: be thankful unto Him and bless His name. For the Lord is good; His mercy is everlasting; and His truth endureth to all generations (Psalms 100:4,5).

We should never come before the Lord with empty hands. It is so important to have an attitude of gratitude and to develop a lifestyle of giving. We give out of a gracious heart.

And they shall not appear before the Lord empty: Every man shall give as he is able, according to the blessing of the Lord by God which He hath given thee (Deut 16:16-17).

Freely ye have received, freely give (Mathew 10:8).

Giving is an act of worship. Worship is not limited to singing or playing music unto God. It is a way of being. We worship with our time, talent, gifts, finances, thoughts, words, attitude, behavior . . . the way we treat each other. It's the way we show honour to the Lord.

Wise men came to worship Jesus: and when they had opened their treasures, they presented unto Him gifts; gold, and frankincense, and myrrh. (Matthew 2:11).

These gifts were symbolic and represented something very meaningful to Jesus: Gold is a symbol of royalty, which signified Jesus' Kingship. Frankincense is an incense used by priests, which represented Jesus' priesthood, His role as our High Priest. Myrrh is a burial spice, which was used to embalm the dead, which prophetically signified that Jesus was born to die.

What we present to the Lord should also be meaningful.

David said, I will not offer to the Lord my God sacrifices that have cost me nothing (2 Samuel 24:24).

Then took Mary a pound of ointment of spikenard, very costly, and anointed the feet of Jesus, and wiped His feet with her hair (John 12:3).

He who is forgiven much, loves much (Luke 8:47).

Verily I say unto you, wheresoever this gospel shall be preached in the whole world, there shall also this, that this woman hath done, be told for a memorial of her (Matthew 26:13).

A man's gift maketh room for him, and bringeth him before great men (Proverbs 18:16).

It pleases God when our worship is authentic. He is interested in our motives and intentions. He looks at the condition of the heart.

God is a Spirit: and they that worship Him must worship Him in spirit and in truth (John 4:24).

When we give the Lord our best, we will also receive His best.

We were not created to be reservoirs. God pours into us to pour out of us. Giving and receiving should be a continuous cycle. As we receive, we should also give. Our ability to give and receive will affect our capacity to experience true prosperity. Anything we hold on to will not benefit us. God honours a heart of gratitude with even more blessings, and will multiply the resources He's given us. He will give more seed to the sower.

Now He that ministereth seed to the sower both minister bread for your food, and multiply your seed sown, and increase the fruits of your righteousness; Being enriched in every thing to all bountifulness, which causeth through us thanksgiving to God. For the administration of this service not only supplieth the want of the saints, but is abundant also by many thanksgivings unto God (2 Corinthians 9:10-12).

Offer God a sacrifice of praise and thanksgiving.

Out of the abundance of the heart the mouth speaketh (Luke 6:45).

Let the redeemed of the Lord say so (Psalm 107:2).

And it came to pass, as he went to Jerusalem through the midst of Samaria and Galilee. And as he entered into a certain village, there met him ten men that were lepers, which stood afar off: And they lifted up their voices, and said, Jesus, master, have mercy on us. And when He saw them, He said unto them, Go shew yourselves unto the priest. And it came to pass, that, as they went, they were cleansed.

And one of them, when he saw that he was healed, turned back, and with a loud voice glorified God. And fell down on his face at His feet, giving Him thanks: and he was a Samaritan. And Jesus answering said, were there not ten cleansed? But where are the nine? There are not found that returned to give glory to God, save this stranger. And He said unto him, Arise, go thy way: thy faith hath made thee whole (Luke 17:15-19).

Thanksgiving will break the power of the enemy. When you give thanks in the midst of difficulty it brings pleasure to God.

David said, I will offer to thee the sacrifice of thanksgiving, and will call upon the name of the Lord (Psalms 116:17).

In everything give thanks: for this is the will of God in Christ Jesus concerning you (1 Thes 5:18).

Beloved, think it not strange concerning the fiery trial which is to try you, as though some strange thing happened to you: But rejoice, inasmuch as ye are partakers of Christ's sufferings; that, when His glory shall be revealed, ye may be glad also with exceeding joy (1Peter 4:12-13).

Ye are a chosen generation, a royal priesthood, an holy nation, a peculiar people; that ye should shew forth the praises of Him who hath called you out of darkness into His marvelous light (1Peter 2:9).

Rejoice in the Lord always: and again I say, Rejoice (Phillipians 4:4).

Give unto the Lord the glory due unto His name; worship the Lord in the beauty of holiness (Psalms 29:2).

Praise ye the Lord. Praise God in His sanctuary; praise Him in the firmament of His power. Praise Him for His mighty acts: praise Him according to His excellent greatness. Let everything that hath breath praise the Lord (Psalms 150: 1,2,6)!!

MONEY

There are many ways to worship and honour the Lord for the blessings He has bestowed upon us, but our finances seem to be the one area that is difficult for many to surrender.

Jesus speaks quite a bit about money in the scriptures, and how it can hinder our spiritual walk if we are not careful.

But they that will be rich fall into temptation and a snare, and into many foolish and hurtful lusts, which drown men in destruction and perdition.

For the love of money is the root of all evil: which while some coveted after, they have erred from the faith, and pierced themselves through with many sorrows. But thou, O man of God, flee these things; and follow after righteousness, godliness, faith, love, patience, meekness (1 Timothy 6:9-11).

Charge them that are rich in this world, that they be not high minded, nor trust in uncertain riches, but in the living God, who giveth us richly all things to enjoy; That they do good, that they be rich in good works, ready to distribute, willing to communicate; Laying up in store for themselves a good foundation against the time to come, that they may lay hold on eternal life (1 Timothy 6:17-19).

No man can serve two masters: for either he will hate the one, and love the other; or else he will hold to the one, and despise the other. Ye cannot serve God and mammon (Matthew 6:24).

For what is a man profited, if he shall gain the whole world, and lose his own soul? Or what shall a man give in exchange for his soul (Matthew 16:26).

From whence come wars and fightings among you? Come they not hence, even of your lusts that war in your members?

Ye lust, and have not: ye kill, and desire to have, and cannot obtain: ye fight and war, yet ye have not, because ye ask not.

Ye ask, and receive not, because ye ask amiss, that ye may consume it upon your lusts (James 4:1-3).

In Luke 18:18, Jesus has an encounter with a rich ruler, who asks Him what He should do to inherit eternal life. Jesus began to list the various commandments, which the ruler said he has kept since his youth. Then Jesus, assessing the condition of his heart, asked him to sell all that he had, distribute the proceeds to the poor, and follow Him. This made the ruler very unhappy. He could not depart without his wealth.

It is very difficult for the rich to enter into the kingdom of God (Luke 18:24).

Because money represents status and security for many, we will often be tested in this area. We will be tested with what we hold most valuable to us.

For where your treasure is, there will be your heart also (Luke 12:34).

God tested Abraham with his son Isaac: Take now thy son, thine only son Isaac, whom thou lovest, and get thee into the land of Moriah; and offer him there for a burnt offering upon one of the mountains which I will tell thee of. (Gen 22:2).

Out of faith, trust, and obedience to God, Abraham followed the Lord's instructions . . . he passed his test. God said, lay not thine hand upon the lad, neither do thou any thing unto him: for now I know that thou fearest God, seeing thou hast not withheld thy son, thine only son from Me (Genesis 22:12).

God was now confident where Abraham's heart was. He is interested in our hearts. He wants all of us!

Because thou hast done this thing, and hast not withheld thy son, thine only son: that in blessing I will bless thee, and in multiplying I will multiply thy seed as the stars of the heaven, and as the sand which is upon the sea shore; and thy seed shall possess the gate of his enemies; And in thy seed shall all the nations of the earth be blessed; because thou hast obeyed my voice (Genesis 22:16-18).

Our obedience to God will always open the door to more blessings.

Mary, Jesus' mother, said to the servants: Whatsoever He saith unto you, do it!

FAITH

God responds to faith. Without it, it is impossible to please Him (Heb 11:6).

He did not many mighty works there because of their unbelief (Mathew 3:58).

Sometimes we look for signs before we take the first step, but signs and wonders will follow the believer (Mark 16:17,20).

Then said Martha unto Jesus, Lord, if thou hadst been here, my brother had not died. But I know, that even now, whatsoever thou wilt ask of God, God will give it thee.

Jesus saith unto her, thy brother shall rise again.

Martha saith unto Him, I know that he shall rise again in the resurrection at the last day.

Jesus said unto her, I am the resurrection, and the life: he that believeth in Me, though he were dead, yet shall he live. Said I not unto thee, that, if thou wouldest believe, thou shouldest see the glory of God (Matthew 11:21-25, 40)?

Be not faithless, but believing (John 20:27).

Blessed are they that have not seen, and yet have believed (John 20:29).

All things are possible to him that believeth (Mark 9:23).

You can receive a miracle from the hand of God right now, if you will only believe.

Behold, I will do a new thing; now it shall spring forth; shall ye not know it? I will even make a way in the wilderness, and rivers in the desert (Isaiah 43:19).

When the Lord presents us with an opportunity to give, it is an opportunity to receive His very best.

When we give out of a thankful and gracious heart, we willingly return a generous portion of our monetary resources to God as an expression of our love, trust, and faith in Him. We believe that He will meet every need according to His riches in glory (Phillipians 4:19).

We should not give out of fear, duty or obligation. God loves a cheerful giver (2 Corinthians 9:7).

Honour the Lord with your wealth and with the best part of everything your land produces (Proverbs 3:9).

Honour the Lord with thy substance, and with the firstfruits of all thine increase: so shall thy barns be filled with plenty, and thy presses shall burst out with new wine (Proverbs 3: 9, 10).

And Jesus sat over against the treasury, and beheld how the people cast money into the treasury: and many that were rich cast in much. And there came a certain poor widow, and she threw in two mites, which make a farthing. And He called unto him His disciples, and saith unto them, Verily I say unto you, That this poor widow hath cast more in, than all they which have cast into the treasury: For all they did cast in of their abundance: but she of her want did cast in all that she had, even all her living (Mark 12:41-44).

The Lord seeth not as man seeth; for man looketh on the outward appearance, but the Lord looketh on the heart (1 Samuel 16:7).

Jesus honoured what the widow gave more than the extravagant offerings of the rich, because she sacrificed all. She trusted Him with all that she had.

What we offer to the Lord should be a reflection of our relationship with Him.

TITHES AND OFFERINGS

Will a man rob God? Yet ye have robbed Me. But ye say, wherein have we robbed thee? In tithes and offerings (Malachi 3:8).

Bring ye all the tithes into the storehouse, that there may be meat in Mine house, and prove Me now herewith, saith the Lord of hosts, if I will not open you the windows of heaven, and pour you out a blessing, that there shall not be room enough to receive it.

And I will rebuke the devourer for your sakes, and he shall not destroy the fruits of your ground; neither shall your vine cast her fruit before the time in the field, saith the Lord of hosts. And all nations shall call you blessed; for ye shall be a delightsome land, saith the Lord of hosts (Malachi 3: 10-12).

Do you not know that they which minister about holy things live of the things of the temple? And they which wait at the altar are partakers with the altar?

Even so hath the Lord ordained that they which preach the gospel should live of the gospel ((1 Corinthians 9: 13,14).

It is reported that only twenty percent of churchgoers tithe. Many say they do not give because they do not have, but according to the measure of faith with which you give, that same measure will be returned to you (Mathew 7:2).

God is not a man that He should lie; neither the son of man, that He should repent: hath He said, and shall He not do it? Or hath He spoken, and shall He not make it good (Numbers 23:19)?

The word of God is quick and powerful, and sharper than any twoedged sword (Hebrews 4:12).

So shall My word be that goeth forth out of My mouth: it shall not return unto Me void, but it shall accomplish that which I please, and it shall prosper in the thing whereto I sent it (Isaiah 55:11).

God is no respector of persons (Acts 10:34). If you give, you will receive.

And when they were come to Capernaum, they that received tribute money came to Peter, and said, doth not your master pay tribute (taxes)? He saith Yes.

Jesus saith unto him, go thou to the sea, and cast an hook, and take up the fish that first cometh up; and when thou hast opened his mouth, thou shalt find a piece of money: that take, and give unto them for me and thee (Matthew 17:24-27).

Your harvest can be manifested through many ways: a creative idea, revelation, wisdom, concepts, open doors, divine appointments, materially, physically, financially . . . One word from God can change your entire life.

The Lord is extremely strategic. He knows your needs and has very creative ways of getting what you need to you. He should not be limited or put into a box. When we act upon His word it will produce results.

When you return your tithes and offerings unto the Lord it also blesses your place of worship. We are to give where we are spiritually fed, and wherever and whenever the Spirit of the Lord directs.

Our monetary gifts help to support the ministry and enables the pastor to serve more effectively, which will ultimately affect the congregation. The church was not designed to take care of itself, in that the burden is left for the head to bear. It takes money to operate a church. Your gifts will also be used to advance the gospel, and to bring hope, peace, salvation, healing, deliverance and restoration to many hurting people. You are investing in souls. We, as the body of Christ, are joined together as one. We are all obligated to do our part. The early church understood this, and there was no lack among them. They were united and full of power. They broke bread together, prayed together, and sold what they had so they could share with those who had more of a need than themselves (Acts 2: 43-47).

There seems to be great controversy over the tithe.

Some will argue that tithing 10% of your earnings is of the old testament. Jesus stated in Mathew 5-17), that He did not come to abolish the law but to fulfill it. The law was fulfilled through love (Hebrews 10:16). We give as an expression of our love, trust, faith and gratitude to the Lord. He can do more with the 10% than we could do with the 100%.

He does not need our money. It all belongs to Him anyway. He will use what we present to Him as a point of contact to bring more blessings to us.

For whatsoever a man soweth, that shall he also reap (Galatians 6:7).

He that observeth the wind shall not sow; and he that regardeth the clouds shall not reap.

In the morning sow thy seed, and in the evening withhold not thine hand (Ecclesiastes 11:4,6).

And the Lord said unto him, what is that in thine hand: And he said, a rod. And He said, cast it on the ground. And he cast it on the ground, and it became a serpent; and Moses fled from before it.

And the Lord said unto Moses, put forth thine hand, and take it by the tail. And he put forth his hand, and caught it, and it became a rod in his hand (Exodus 4:2-4).

God had to demonstrate to Moses that what he had in his hand could not accomplish much. But when Moses obeyed the Lord's instructions, what he had in his hand came alive. God breathed life into it. He will also take your dead seed and breathe life into it. He will do exceeding abundantly above all that you can ask or think according to the power that worketh in you (Ephesians 3:20).

AGREEMENT

Behold, there came a certain ruler, and worshipped Him, saying, my daughter is even now dead: but come and lay thy hand upon her, and she shall live.

And when Jesus came into the ruler's house, and saw the minstrels and the people making noise, He said unto them, Give place; for the maid is not dead, but sleepeth. And they laughed Him to scorn. But when the people were put forth, He went in, and took her by the hand, and the maid arose (Matthew 9:18, 23-25).

Two cannot walk unless they agree. Jesus needed agreement, so He put out all the unbelievers and shut the door. An unbelieving heart will hinder you. Come into alignment and agreement with the Lord for your miracle today.

After the disciples fished all night and caught nothing, Jesus instructed them to cast their net on the right side. They cast therefore, and now they were not able to draw it for the multitude of fishes (Matthew 21:6,7).

When we enter into partnership and agreement with the Lord, we cease from our self-effort and dead works. There is no longer a need to strive or toil. We work smarter, not harder.

TRUST

After Jesus trained His twelve disciples and was ready to send them out, He asked them not to take anything with them. He wanted them to rely solely on Him for their provisions.

These twelve Jesus sent forth, and commanded them, saying, provide neither gold, nor silver, nor brass in your purses, nor scrip for your journey, neither two coats, neither shoes, nor yet staves: for the workman is worthy of his meat (Matthew 10:5,9,10).

The Lord expects us to have that same faith and trust in Him, for He knows what we are in need of before we ask Him (Matthew 6:8).

But my God shall supply all your need according to His riches in glory by Christ Jesus (Phillipians 4:19).

And when it was evening, His disciples came to Him saying, this is a desert place, and the time is now past; send the multitude away, that they may go into the villages, and buy themselves victuals (food).
But Jesus said unto them, they need not depart; give ye them to eat. And they said unto Him, we have here but five loaves, and two fishes. He said, bring them hither to me.

He commanded the multitude to sit down on the grass, and took the five loaves, and the two fishes, and looking up to heaven, He blessed, and brake, and gave the loaves to His disciples, and the disciples to the multitude.

And they did all eat, and were filled: and they took up of the fragments and remained twelve baskets full. And they had eaten were about five thousand men, beside women and children (Matthew 14: 15-21).

When Jesus told His disciples to feed the multitude, He was trying to get them to shift their thinking from the natural to the supernatural. In the natural it was impossible to feed over 5,000 people with only five loaves of bread and two fishes, but with God, all things are possible. The blessing and breaking of the bread was a shadowing of Jesus' crucifixion. It represented His body which would be broken on the cross as the ultimate sacrifice for the world. He is the bread of life! Sitting represents a state of relaxation. When we understand that God is our Source of supply, we don't need to worry, we are confident that He will take care of our every need.

God intends for His children to live in the overflow. To truly experience the abundant life in Him, where there is nothing wanting, nothing needed and nothing broken . . . to be whole and complete in Him.

The Lord is my Sheppard, I shall not want (Psalms 23:1)!!

Chapter 7

GIVING YOUR HEART TO GOD

REPENT YE: FOR THE *kingdom of heaven is at hand (Matthew 3:2).*

Repent ye therefore, and be converted, that your sins may be blotted out, when the times of refreshing shall come from the presence of the Lord (Acts 3:19).

If My people, which are called by My name, shall humble themselves, and pray, and seek My face, and turn from their wicked ways; then will I hear from heaven, and will forgive their sin, and will heal their land.

I am the Lord that healeth thee (Exodus 15:26).

I am the Lord, I change not (Malachi 3:6).

Now Mine eyes shall be open, and Mine ears attent unto the prayer that is made in this place. For now have I chosen and sanctified this house, that My name may be there for ever: and Mine eyes and mine heart shall be there perpetually (2 Chronicles 7:14,15).

Then shall ye call upon Me, and ye shall go and pray unto Me, and I will hearken unto you. And ye shall seek Me, and find Me, when ye shall search for Me with all your heart. And I will be found of you, saith the Lord: and I will turn away your captivity (Jeremiah 29:12-14).

I, even I, am He who blots out your transgressions, for My own sake, and remembers your sins no more (Isaiah 43:25).

Incline your ear, and come unto Me: hear, and your soul shall live; and I will make an everlasting covenant with you (Isaiah 55:3).

As far as the east is from the west, so far hath He removed our transgressions from us (Psalms 103:12).

For we have not an high priest which cannot be touched with the feeling of our infirmities; but was in all points tempted like as we are, yet without sin. Let us therefore come boldly unto the throne of grace, that we may obtain mercy, and find grace to help in time of need (Hebrews4:15-16).

There is no sin that is too great nor pit too deep. Is there anything that is too hard for the Lord? He is God all by Himself. He, who spoke the world into existence, and commanded the storm to be still.
Nothing is impossible for Him!

For He spoke and it was done; He commanded, and it stood fast (Psalms 33:9).

Who hath ascended up into heaven, or descended? Who hath gathered the wind in His fists? Who hath bound the waters in a garment? Who hath established all the ends of the earth? What is His name, and what is His Son's name, if thou canst tell (Proverbs 30:4)?

Be still and know that He is God. Enter into His rest and trust Him. Lean not on your own understanding, for He will surely bring it to pass.

Behold, the Lord's hand is not shortened, that it cannot save; neither His ear heavy, that it cannot hear (Isaiah 59:1).

The Lord will give strength unto His people; the Lord will bless His people with peace (Psalm 29:11).

Every word of God is pure: He is a shield unto them that put their trust in Him (Proverbs 30:5).

ARISE!

Arise, shine; for thy light is come, and the glory of the Lord is risen upon thee (Isaiah 60:1).

And when he came to himself he said, I will arise and go to my Father. And he arose, and came to his Father. But when he was yet a great way off, his Father saw him, and had compassion, and ran, and fell on his neck, and kissed him (Luke 15:18, 20).

Your heavenly Father is waiting for you with open arms.

In thee, O Lord, do I put my trust; let me never be ashamed: deliver me in thy righteousness. Bow down thine ear to me; deliver me speedily: be thou my strong rock, for an house of defence to save me (Psalms 31:1,2).

As the hart panteth after the water brooks, so panteth my soul after thee, O God. My soul thirsteth for God, for the living God (Psalms 42: 1,2).

I will lift up mine eyes unto the hills, from whence cometh my help. My help cometh from the Lord, which made heaven and earth. He will not suffer thy foot to be moved: He that keepeth thee will not slumber (Psalms 121: 1-3).

I waited patiently for the Lord, and He inclined unto me, and heard my cry. He brought me up also out of an horrible pit, out of the miry clay, and set my feet upon a rock, and established my goings. And He hath put a new song in my mouth, even praise unto our God: many shall see it, and fear, and shall trust in the Lord (Psalms 40: 1, 2).

I will extol thee, O Lord; for thou has lifted me up, and hast not made my foes to rejoice over me. O Lord my God, I cried unto thee, and thou hast healed me (Psalms 30: 1,2).

Thy word will I keep in my heart that I may not sin against you (Psalm 119:11).

Search me, O God, and know my heart: try me, and know my thoughts: And see if there be any wicked way in me, and lead me in the way everlasting (Psalm 139:23-24).

Thy word is a lamp unto my feet, and a light unto my path (Psalm 119: 105).

Unto the upright there ariseth light in the darkness (Psalms 112:4).

I will praise thee, O Lord, with my whole heart; I will shew forth all thy marvelous works (Psalms 9:1).

They that wait upon the Lord shall renew their strength; they shall mount up with wings as eagles; they shall run, and not be weary; and they shall walk, and not faint (Isaiah 40:31).

Wait on the Lord, be of good courage, and He shall strengthen thine heart: wait, I say, on the Lord (Psalms 27:14).

Keep thy heart with all diligence; for out of it are the issues of life (Proverbs 4:23).

Cast not away therefore your confidence, which hath great recompence of reward (Hebrews 10:35).

He that cometh to God must believe that He is, and that He is a rewarder of them that diligently seek Him (Hebrews 11:6).

God resisteth the proud, but giveth grace unto the humble. Submit yourselves therefore to God. Resist the devil, and he will flee from you. Draw nigh to God, and He will draw nigh to you. Humble yourselves in the sight of the Lord, and He shall lift you up (James 4: 6-8,10).

And it shall come to pass in that day, that his burden shall be taken away from off his shoulder, and his yoke from off his neck, and the yoke shall be destroyed because of the anointing (Isaiah 10:27).

Stand fast therefore in the liberty wherewith Christ hath made us free, and be not entangled again with the yoke of bondage (Galatians 5:1).

Therefore thou shalt keep the commandments of the Lord thy God, to walk in His ways, and to fear (respect, reverence) Him.

For the Lord thy God bringeth thee into a good land, a land of brooks of water, of fountains and depths that spring out of the valleys and hills; a land of wheat, and barley, and vines, and fig trees, and pomegranates; a land of oil olive, and honey;

A land wherein thou shalt eat bread without scarceness, thou shalt not lack anything in it (Deut. 8: 5-9).

O taste and see that the Lord is good: blessed is the man that trusteth in Him. O fear the Lord, ye His saints: for there is no want to them that fear Him (Psalms 34:8-9).

Blessed is everyone that feareth the Lord; that walketh in His ways (Psalms 128:1).

Therefore whosoever heareth these sayings of Mine, and doeth them, I will liken him unto a wise man, which built his house upon a rock (Matthew 7: 24-25).

Except the Lord build the house, they labour in vain that build it (Psalms 127:1).

If ye continue in My word, then are ye My disciples indeed; And ye shall know the truth, and the truth shall make you free (John 8:31-32).

These things I have spoken unto you, that in Me ye might have peace. In the world ye shall have tribulation: but be of good cheer; I have overcome the world (John 16:33).

Jesus is the Christ, the Son of God; and that believing ye might have life through His name (John 20:31).

When we truly give our hearts to the Lord, we have access to life, healing, favour, peace, love, joy, wisdom, power . . . we position ourselves to receive all that He has and all that He is. We become heirs with Him and one with His Spirit. We enter into alignment and agreement with Him, tapping into unlimited provisions for our every need. No good thing will He withhold from those who walk upright before Him (Psalms 84:11).

Delight thyself also in the Lord; and He shall give thee the desires of thine heart (Psalm 37:4).

Therefore I say unto you, take no thought for your life, what ye shall eat, or what ye shall drink; nor yet for your body, what ye shall put on. Is not the life more than meat, and the body than raiment?

Wherefore, if God so clothe the grass of the field, which to day is, and to morrow is cast into the oven, shall He not much more clothe you?

Seek ye first the kingdom of God, and His righteousness; and all these things shall be added unto you.

Take therefore no thought for the morrow: for the morrow shall take thought for the things of itself (Matthew 6: 25, 30, 32-34).

We have been given everything pertaining to life and godliness, through the knowledge of Him that hath called us to glory and virtue (2 Peter 1:3).

Blessed be the God and Father of our Lord Jesus Christ, who hath blessed us with all spiritual blessings in heavenly places in Christ (Ephesians 1:3).

We don't have to look on the outside for what we already possess on the inside. We are complete in Him (Colossians 2:10).

It is God's will for us to prosper in every area of our lives. It is not about gimmicks, formulas, religion, tradition or good works, but simply receiving by faith what has already been provided by grace.

Thou art ever with Me, and all that I have is thine (Luke 15: 31).

When we begin to shift our thinking from the natural to the supernatural, we begin to move beyond the point of blessing into a place where we are walking in His miracle-working power, by pressing deeper in to a spiritual walk with Him.

The Spirit of the Lord is saying to His children today:

Labour not for the meat which perisheth, but for that meat which endureth unto everlasting life, which the Son of man shall give unto you: for Him hath God the Father sealed.
For the bread of God is He which cometh down from heaven, and giveth life unto the world.
I am the bread of life, he that cometh to me shall never hunger; and he that believeth on Me shall never thirst (John 6:27,33,35).

WHAT ARE YOU THIRSTY FOR?

There is a special place in our hearts that is reserved for our creator. There is nothing that can fill it . . . no substitutes. There is nothing that can sustain us like the Bread of life, nothing that can quench our thirsty souls like the Living Water, nothing that can meet our every need like the great I AM . . . Jesus Christ is His name, and His glory He will not share with another!

That special place in our hearts can only be filled by Jesus. It cannot be filled by people, substance, money, status, possessions . . . only He can fill the void. Until we enter into a personal relationship with our creator, we will continue to be dissatisfied with anything less. We were created for Him!

Whosoever drinketh of this water shall thirst again: But whosoever drinketh of the water that I shall give him shall never thirst; but the water that I shall give him shall be in him a well of water springing up into everlasting life (John 4: 13,14).

Come unto Me, all ye that labour and are heavy laden, and I will give you rest. Take My yoke upon you, and learn of Me; for I am meek and lowly in heart: and ye shall find rest unto your souls. For My yoke is easy, and My burden is light (Matthew 11: 28-30).

My grace is sufficient for thee: for My strength is made perfect in weakness (2 Corinthians 12:9).

Peace I leave with you, My peace I give unto you: not as the world giveth, give I unto you. Let not your heart be troubled, neither let it be afraid (John 14:27).

Call unto Me, and I will answer thee, and shew thee great and mighty things, which thou knowest not (Jeremiah 33:3).

The secret things belong unto the Lord our God: but those things which are revealed belong unto us and to our children for ever, that we may do all the words of this law (Deut. 29:29).

REACH OUT AND TOUCH HIM

And behold, a woman, which was diseased with an issue of blood twelve years, came behind Him, and touched the hem of His garment: For she said within herself, if I may but touch His garment, I shall be whole.

But Jesus turned Him about, and when He saw her, He said, daughter, be of good comfort; thy faith hath made thee whole. And the woman was made whole from that hour (Matthew 9:20-22).

Wilt thou be made whole (John 5:6)?

Rise, take up thy bed and walk (John 5:8)!!

Believe God. Take hold and receive everything He has for you. We will not possess anything we are not willing to pursue. Pursue your healing, pursue your blessing, pursue God today!

There was in a city a judge, which feared not God, neither regarded man: And there was a widow in that city; and she came unto him, saying, avenge me of mine adversary. And he would not for a while: but afterward he said within himself, though I fear not God, nor regard man; Yet because this widow troubleth me, I will avenge her, lest by her continual coming she weary me. And the Lord said, Hear what the unjust judge saith. And shall not God avenge his own elect, which cry day and night unto Him, though He bear long with them? I tell you that He will avenge them speedily. Nevertheless when the Son of man cometh, shall He find faith on the earth (Luke 18:2-8)?

From the days of John the Baptist until now the kingdom of heaven suffereth violence, and the violent take it by force (Matthew 11:12).

WHAT WENT YE OUT INTO THE WILDERNESS TO SEE?

Behold the Lamb of God!!!

When Jesus came into the coasts of Caesarea Philippi, He asked His disciples, saying, whom do men say that I the Son of man am?

And they said, some say that thou art John the Baptist: some, Elias; and others, Jeremias or one of the prophets. He saith unto them, But whom say ye that I am?

And Simon Peter answered and said, thou art the Christ, the Son of the living God. And Jesus answered and said unto him, blessed art thou, Simon Barjona: for flesh and blood hath not revealed it unto thee, but my Father which is in heaven (Matthew 16:13-17).

We all need a personal revelation of who God is. A personal experience of His love, power and goodness. Not just head knowledge, He must be revealed in us and to us by the Holy Spirit.

Now we believe, not because of thy saying: for we have heard Him ourselves, and know that this is indeed the Christ, the Savior of the world (John 4:42).

For God, who commanded the light to shine out of darkness, hath shined in our hearts, to give the light of the knowledge of the glory of God in the face of Jesus Christ (2 Corinthians 4:6).

That we may know Him, and the power of His resurrection (Philippians 3:10).

THE GREAT "I AM"

Come now therefore, and I will send thee unto Pharaoh, that thou mayest bring forth My people the children of Israel out of Egypt.

And Moses said unto God, who am I, that I should go unto Pharaoh, and that I should bring forth the children of Israel out of Egypt?

And Moses said unto God, behold, when I come unto the children of Israel, and shall say unto them, the God of your fathers hath sent me unto you; and they shall say to me, what is his name? What shall I say unto them?

And God said unto Moses, I AM THAT I AM: and He said, thus shalt say unto the children of Israel I AM hath sent me unto you (Exodus 3:10,13,14).

He is the great I AM. He is everything that we need Him to be.

WILL YOU RECEIVE HIM?

Let not your heart be troubled. Ye believe in God believe also in Me (John 14:1)

I am the resurrection, and the life: he that believeth in Me, though he were dead, yet shall he live: and whosoever liveth and believeth in Me shall never die (2 Corinthians 12:9).

We have been given a great gift in Jesus. In order to walk in it, we must first receive it by faith. When we totally surrender our all to the Lord, He will make something beautiful out of us and use us for His glory. We will become transformed by His love.

And Jesus entered and passed through Jericho. And, behold, there was a man named Zacchaeus, which was the chief among the publicans, and he was rich.

And he sought to see Jesus who He was; and could not for the press (crowd), because he was little of stature.

And he ran before, and climbed up into a sycamore tree to see Him: for he was to pass that way. And when Jesus came to the place, He looked up, and saw him, and said unto him, Zacchaeus, make haste, and come down; for today I must abide at thy house.

And he made haste, and came down, and received Him joyfully. And Jesus said unto him, this day is salvation come to this house, for the Son of man is come to seek and to save that which was lost (Luke 19: 1-6, 9-10).

How think ye? If a man have an hundred sheep, and one of them be gone astray, doth he not leave the ninety and nine, and goeth into the mountains, and seeketh that which is gone astray?

And if so be that he find it, verily I say unto you, he rejoiceth more of that sheep, than of the ninety and nine which went not astray.

Even so it is not the will of your Father which is in heaven that one of these little ones should perish (Matthew 18:11-14).

Behold, I stand at the door, and knock: if any man hear My voice, and open the door, I will come in to him, and will sup with him, and he with Me (Revelation 3:20).

Now therefore fear the Lord, and serve Him in sincerity and in truth: and put away the gods which your fathers served; And if it seem evil unto you to serve the Lord, choose you this day whom ye will serve: But as for me and my house, we will serve the Lord (Joshua 24:14-15).

The Lord is knocking at the door of your heart. Will you let Him in? Go ahead, I dare you. I dare you to be radically blessed!

FINAL THOUGHTS

God has a plan and a great purpose for our lives. He knows everything about us: *Before I formed thee in the belly I knew thee; and before thou camest forth out of the womb I sanctified thee (Jeremiah 1:5). The thoughts that I think towards you are thoughts of peace, and not of evil, to give you an expected end (Jeremiah 29:11). You are fearfully and wonderfully made (Psalm 139:14).*

Fear thou not; for I am with thee: be not dismayed; for I am thy God: I will strengthen thee; yea, I will help thee; yea, I will uphold thee with the right hand of My righteousness (Isaiah 41:10).

When we seek first God's kingdom and His way of doing things, all that we are in need of will be provided for us. We were not created to meet our own needs. All of our needs are met in Christ. In Him we live, move, and have our being (Acts 17:28). God knows our needs and will meet them according to His riches in glory by Christ Jesus. The joy of the Lord is our strength (Nehemiah 8:10). When we are weak, then we are strong in Him (2 Corinthians 12:10).

Cast all your cares upon Him; because He cares for you (1 Peter 5:7).

Give Him your failures, give Him your pain. Give Him your pleasures and your success. Give Him your past, give Him your present, give Him your future. Give, give, give! Why? Because, all things work together for good to them that love God, to them who are called according to His purpose (Romans 8:28).

Jesus is the way, allow Him to direct your steps. He is the truth, renew your mind with His word. He is the life, our only true source of supply. He is the solution to every situation, challenge and obstacle we face in life, and the answer and key to our prosperity.

The abundant life cannot be experienced apart from Him. He is the vine, we are the branches (John 15:5). We draw life from Him. We tap into His supernatural resource by staying connected to Him with all our heart, mind and soul. He is the life giver and sustainer, in Him there is no lack!!!

We are here to fulfill our destiny in Christ, to take our rightful position in Him, and allow Him to live in and through us. We are called to be a living testimony of His awesome love, and to testify that His grace truly is sufficient for us all. Greater is He that is within than he that is in the world (1John 4:4).

Blessed is everyone that feareth (reverence, respect) the Lord; that walketh in His ways (Psalm 128:1).

Blessed are they that do His commandments, that they may have right to the tree of life (Revelation 22:14).

PRAYER FOR REDEDICATION

Heavenly Father,

You are my light and my salvation, unto You do I lift up my soul. Have mercy upon me, according to Your lovingkindness: according unto the multitude of Your tender mercies blot out my transgressions.

Create in me a clean heart; and renew a right spirit within me. Restore unto me the joy of Your salvation, and uphold me with Your righteous right hand;

You are the rock of my salvation and the strength of my life. I submit myself completely unto You and I receive You as Lord and Master of my life.

Teach me Your ways and lead me in a plain path. Help me to walk in the light of Your word and lean not on my own understanding. Your word is a light unto my feet and a lamp unto my path.

Let Your perfect will be done in my life. In Jesus name I pray, Amen!

THE GREAT I AM

1. Jehova-Rohi The Lord our Sheppard

2. Jehovah-Jireh The Lord our provider

3. Jehovah-Nissi The Lord our Banner

4. Jehovah-Rapha The Lord our Healer

5. Jehovah-Shalom The Lord our Peace

1 CORINTHIANS 13

Though I speak with the tongues of men and of angels, and have not charity (love), I am become as sounding brass, or a tinkling cymbal.

And though I have the gift of prophecy, and understand all mysteries, and all knowledge; and though I have all faith, so that I could remove mountains, and have not charity, I am nothing.

And though I bestow all my goods to feed the poor, and though I give my body to be burned, and have not charity, it profiteth me nothing.

Charity suffereth long, and is kind; charity envieth not; charity vaunteth not itself, is not puffed up, doth not behave itself unseemly, seeketh not her own, is not easily provoked, thinketh no evil; rejoiceth not in iniquity, but rejoiceth in the truth; beareth all things, believeth all things, hopeth all things, endureth all things.

Charity never faileth: but whether there be prophecies, they shall fail; whether there be tongues they shall cease; whether there be knowledge, it shall vanish away.

For we know in part, and we prophecy in part. But when that which is perfect is come, then that which is in part shall be done away.

When I was a child, I spake as a child, I understood as a child, I thought as a child: but when I became a man, I put away childish things.

For now we see through a glass, darkly; but then face to face: now I know in part; but then shall I know even as also I am known.

And now abideth faith, hope, charity, these three; but the greatest of these is charity.

THE BEATITUDES

Blessed are the poor in spirit: for theirs is the kingdom of heaven.

Blessed are they that mourn: for they shall be comforted.

Blessed are the meek: for they shall inherit the earth.

Blessed are they which do hunger and thirst after righteousness: for they shall be filled.

Blessed are the merciful: for they shall obtain mercy.

Blessed are the pure in heart: for they shall see God.

Blessed are the peacemakers: for they shall be called the children of God.

Blessed are they which are persecuted for righteousness' sake: for theirs is the kingdom of heaven.

Blessed are ye, when men shall revile you, and persecute you, and shall say all manner of evil against you falsely, for My sake.

Rejoice, and be exceeding glad: for great is your reward in heaven: for so persecuted they the prophets which were before you.

Ye are the salt of the earth: but if the salt have lost his savour, wherewith shall it be salted? It is thenceforth good for nothing, but to be cast out, and to be trodden under foot of men.

Ye are the light of the world. A city that is set on a hill cannot be hid.

Neither do men light a candle, and put it under a bushel, but on a candlestick, and it giveth light unto all that are in the house.

Let your light so shine before men, that they may see your good works, and glorify your Father which is in heaven.

Think not that I am come to destroy the law, or the prophets: I am not come to destroy, but to fulfill.

For verily I say unto you, Till heaven and earth pass, one jot or one tittle shall in no wise pass from the law, till all be fulfilled.

Whosoever therefore shall break one of these least commandments, and shall teach men so, he shall be called the least in the kingdom of heaven: but whosoever shall do and teach them, the same shall be called great in the kingdom of heaven.

For I say unto you, That except your righteousness shall exceed the righteousness of the scribes and Pharisees, ye shall in no case enter into the kingdom of heaven.

PSALM 23

The Lord is my Sheppard; I shall not want. He maketh me to lie down in green pastures: He leadeth me beside the still waters. He restores my soul:

He leadeth me in the paths of righteousness for His name's sake. *Yea, though I walk through the valley of the shadow of death, I will fear no evil: for thou art with me; thy rod and thy staff they comfort me.*

Thou preparest a table before me in the presence of mine enemies: thou anointest my head with oil; my cup runneth over. Surely goodness and mercy shall follow me all the days of my life: and I will dwell in the house of the Lord forever.

PSALM 27

The Lord is my light and my salvation; whom shall I fear? The Lord is the strength of my life; of whom shall I be afraid? When the wicked, even mine enemies and my foes, came upon me to eat up my flesh, they stumbled and fell. Thou an host should encamp against me, my heart shall not fear: though war should rise against me, in this will I be confident. One thing have I desired of the Lord, that will I seek after; that I may dwell in the house of the Lord, and to inquire in His temple.

For in the time of trouble He shall hide me in His pavilion: in the secret of His tabernacle shall He hide me; He shall set me up upon a rock. And now shall mine head be lifted up above mine enemies round about me: therefore will I offer in His tabernacle sacrifices of joy; I will sing, yea, I will sing praises unto the Lord.

Hear O Lord, when I cry with my voice: have mercy also upon me, and answer me. *When thou saidst seek ye My face; my heart said unto thee, thy face Lord, will I seek.*

Hide not thy face far from me; put not thy servant away in anger: thou hast been my help; leave me not, neither forsake me, O God of my salvation. When my father and my mother forsake me, then the Lord will take me up. Teach me thy way, O Lord, and lead me in a plain path, because of mine enemies. Deliver me not over unto the will of mine enemies: for false witnesses are risen up against me, and such as breathe out cruelty. I had fainted, unless I had believed to see the goodness of the Lord in the land of the living. Wait on the Lord, be of good courage, and He shall strengthen thine heart: wait, I say, on the Lord.

PSALM 91

He that dwelleth in the secret place of the most High shall abide under the shadow of the Almighty. I will say of the Lord, He is my refuge and my fortress: my God; in Him will I trust. Surely He shall deliver thee from the snare of the fowler, and from the noisome pestilence. He shall cover thee with His feathers, and under His wings shalt thou trust:

His truth shall be thy shield and buckler. Thou shalt not be afraid for the terror by night; nor for the arrow that flieth by day; nor for the pestilence that walketh in darkness; nor for the destruction that wasteth at noonday. A thousand shall fall at thy side, and ten thousand at thy right hand; but it shall not come nigh thee. Only with thine eyes shalt thou behold and see the reward of the wicked. *Because thou hast made the Lord, which is my refuge, even the most High, thy habitation;* there shall no evil befall thee neither shall any plague come nigh thy dwelling. For He shall give His angels charge over thee, to keep thee in all thy ways. They shall bear thee up in their hands, lest thou dash thy foot against a stone.

Thou shalt tread upon the lion and adder: the young lion and the dragon shalt thou trample under feet. Because he hath set his love upon Me, therefore will I delive him: I will set him on high, because he hath known My name. He shall call upon Me, and I will answer him: I will be with him in trouble; I will deliver him, and honour him. With long life will I satisfy him, and shew him My salvation.

PSALM 34

I will bless the Lord at all times: His praise shall continually be in my mouth. My soul shall make her boast in the Lord: the humble shall hear thereof, and be glad. O magnify the Lord with me, and let us exalt His name together. I sought the Lord, and He heard me, and delivered me from all my fears. They looked unto Him, and were lightened: and their faces were not ashamed. This poor man cried, and the Lord heard him, and saved him out of all his troubles. The angel of the Lord encampeth round about them that fear him, and delivereth them. O taste and see that the Lord is good: *blessed is the man that trusteth in Him.* O fear the Lord, ye His saints: for *there is no want to them that fear Him.*

The young lions do lack, and suffer hunger: but they that seek the Lord shall not want any good thing. Come, ye children, hearken unto Me: I will teach you the fear of the Lord. What man is he that desireth life, and loveth many days, that he may see good? Keep thy tongue from evil, and thy lips from speaking guile. Depart from evil, and do good; seek peace, and pursue it. The eyes of the Lord are upon the righteous, and His ears are open unto their cry. The face of the Lord is against them that do evil, to cut off the remembrance of them from the earth. The righteous cry, and heareth, and delivereth them out of all their troubles.

The Lord is nigh unto them that are of a broken heart; and saveth such as be of a contrite spirit. *Many are the afflictions of the righteous: but the Lord delivereth him out of them all.* He keepeth all his bones: not one of them is broken. Evil shall slay the wicked: and they that hate the righteous shall be desolate. *The Lord redeemeth the soul of His servants: and none of them that trust in Him shall be desolate.*

DEUTERONOMY 28

And it shall come to pass, if thou shalt hearken diligently unto the voice of the Lord thy God, to observe and to do all His commandments which I command thee this day, that the Lord thy God will set thee on high above all nations of the earth:

And all these blessings shall come on thee, and overtake thee, if thou shalt hearken unto the voice of the Lord thy God. Blessed shalt thou be in the city, and blessed shalt thou be in the field. Blessed shall be the fruit of thy body, and the fruit of thy cattle, the increase of thy kine, and the flocks of thy sheep.

Blessed shall be thy basket and thy store. Blessed shalt thou be when thou comest in, and blessed shalt thou be when thou goest out. The Lord shall cause thine enemies that rise up against thee to be smitten before thy face: they shall come out against thee one way, and flee before thee seven ways.

The Lord shall command the blessing upon thee in thy storehouses, and in all that thou settest thine hand unto; and He shall bless thee in the land which the Lord thy God giveth thee. The Lord shall establish thee an holy people unto Himself, as He hath sworn unto thee, if thou shalt keep the commandments of the Lord thy God, and walk in His ways.

And all people of the earth shall see that thou art called by the name of the Lord; and they shall be afraid of thee. And the Lord shall make thee plenteous in goods, in the fruit of thy body, and in the fruit of thy cattle, and in the fruit of thy ground, in the land which the Lord sware unto thy fathers to give thee.

The Lord shall open unto thee His good treasure, the heaven to give the rain unto thy land in His season, and to bless all the work of thine hand: and thou shalt lend unto many nations, and thou shalt not borrow. And the Lord shall make thee the head, and not the tail; and thou shalt be above only, and thou shalt not be beneath; if that thou hearken unto the commandments of the Lord thy God, which I command thee this day, to observe and to do them:

And thou shalt not go aside from any of the words which I command thee this day, to the right hand, or to the left, to go after other gods to serve them.

NUMBERS 6: 24-26

The Lord bless thee, and keep thee:

The Lord make His face shine upon thee, and be gracious unto thee:

The Lord lift up His countenance upon thee, and give thee peace.

GRATITUDE LIST

NOTES

CONTACT INFORMATION

If you have been blessed by this book and would like to place an order for more copies, share your testimony, or provide feedback, please contact:

jewellfairweatherjones@live.com

If you have been blessed and would like to be a blessing financially, please forward all monetary gifts to:

Pastor Mark Anthony Baxter:

Faith Miracle Temple Inc.
280 Yorkland Blvd
Toronto, Ontario
M2J 1R5

Pastor_mbaxter@hotmail.com